Continent of Ghosts

Also by Bill Bradd

Poetry
Holy Trinity
A Kingdom of Old Men

Prose
Notebooks from the Emerald Triangle

Spoken Word CDs
I Tried To Sing In My Grandfather's Voice
New Work
Continent of Ghosts

Editor
Western Edge: 33 Poets, with Sharon Doubiago and Duane
BigEagle
Mendocino Review

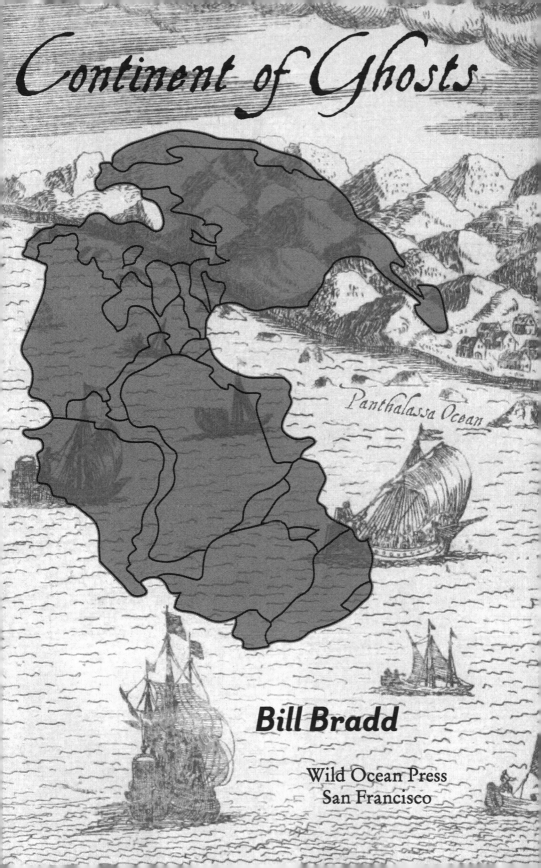

Continent of Ghosts

Panthalassa Ocean

Bill Bradd

Wild Ocean Press
San Francisco

Book cover design by Theresa Whitehill, *Colored Horse Studios*

Credits: Front Cover
- Frame: Public Domain, courtesy of the British Library
- Mirage at Sea, from "The Half Hour Library of Travel, Nature and Science for young readers" James Nisbet & Co., 1896; courtesy of the British Library
- Globe: Opening of the Atlantic; First known illustration of the Opening of the Atlantic Ocean, by Antonio Snider-Pellegrini, 1858. Scan by User:Geoz 2005. Wikimedia Commons, Public Domain

Credits: Title Page
- Sailing Ships and Shoreline: Public Domain, courtesy of the British Library
- Pangaea Map: By en:User:Kieff - File:Pangaea continents.png, CC BY-SA 3.0, https://commons.wikimedia.org/w/index.php?curid=8161694

Author photo courtesy of the author

Bill Bradd
Continent of Ghosts by Bill Bradd

ISBN: 978-1-941137-09-3

Printed in the United States of America on 30% recycled paper

Distributed by Small Press Distribution, Inc., Berkeley, CA
http://www.spdbooks.org

Wild Ocean Press
San Francisco, CA
www.wildoceanpress.com

For Elinore And The Way We Used to Be

...Men see differently. I can best report only from my own wilderness...the important thing is that each man possess such a wilderness and that he consider what marvels are to be observed there.

...Loren Eiseley

But one is aware that there are thoughts more elevated than those that spring from human intelligence; in the first place because of the persons involved and then because of the circumstances. That look binds them together in an eternal friendship.

...Comte de Lautreamont, *Maldoror*

Contents

FOREWARD

When you are born you are one entity, one body, a single geography with future boundaries, shoals, beaches, mountains and mud-holes; one continent if you will, Pangaea, which emerges from the Panthalassa ocean, the salt water of the womb.

As you move through time, though, Pangaea begins to break apart and new continents are formed. You will move under a series of archways so vast that you don't notice until later. You move from Youth to Middle Age and who noticed, except one day you are in a new place with unknown shoals and mud-holes. Time passes, then you are an Elder, where even cutting your fingernails is difficult due to arthritis.

One of these new places within you is what I call the Continent of Ghosts, where all the people you used to know reside now. Some have passed away, moved away or walked away, but they still live within you even though no longer present. Except when you travel to their place via the Appian Way, 365 miles of memories.

To make this project viable to me, I decided to investigate the ghost of my mother, who passed away when I was two and of whom I have no memory. The problem was I was dealing with a cipher, a ghost, needing to avoid Loki the trickster. I began to inspect the blood memory for any scent, any sound, any bird, aslant, any clue. I worked all the senses for any dried rubber-boot pattern. I tried to draw forth any shadow of memory from the distant galaxy of my mind.

PROLOGUE

"Aeneas sang the stray moon and the toiling sun."

The Aeneid

Even as a kid I lived a frontier life. Now, at this late date I realize the frontier that I was living on was at the far edge of the ghost of my mother, deceased when I was two. I searched through the brambles, the early confusion about who I was. The erratic outlaw blunders I made all took place on the frontier of a mind with a vague memory. I knew early on that I was going to search alone, I just didn't know why, but I'd wander off, working the edge, betting it all. On the frontier of the mind, you are so alone that you enjoy the company of ghosts. The difficulty is keeping the dialogue lucid.

There is a void when a loved one leaves.
An empty thing with an edge has grown within you
When a loved one leaves
the edge of
a narrow spine high above coherence
will be the frontier
where you will need to settle
and learn new survival skills.
Pray that you are young
for you will learn so well.

We were born in the Panthalassa Ocean, in the womb of
our mothers, adrift in the salt
of cleansing. Cracks and fissures that would pull us apart lay ahead,
somewhere past the white gauze curtain.
The armature is forming, information comes at a quickening pace,
every edge was a shore, every shore had sea birds, a sprightly dance
and a rackety mess at sundown.
At last we are ready to pass through and declare in an undecipherable
cry, I am here,

        of ancient earth
        I am called Pangaea.

Panthalassa Ocean

The seabirds gather on a certain rock
before the incoming storm.
All the signs are there
no horizon line, a tree
melding to the shades of gray
like separated jigsaw pieces, suddenly it comes together
the picture is now crystal clear, antiseptic, crystal clear.
Nine is the fatal number of air bubbles
the breath of the Panthalassa Sea is long and on the ninth beat
it's all going to be about the edge of things.

>   of places
>   of you and me
>   edges of fear
>   of approximation

edge of land, edge of sea, edge of fire,
edge of yours and mine.
There's an incoming storm
all the seabirds have gathered on one rock.

When the small black sea-birds leave the harbor for the last time
they stop at the kelp bed, splashing, cleaning up, demonstrating
an ancient leaving pattern
unknown to us.
They start to fly, heads thrust forward
wings working
out into the slow breeze
heading north.
Strange, exotic voices rise up from the bedground
my voice calling
my voice calling
I use the ancient tongue.
I will meet you, I shout. I will meet you where
the sun meets the sea.
But first I must perfect my dance steps, the leaving pattern
performed on a bouncing stage of light.

I do not want to speak your language, I want to speak aloud
the language of the insane, where I see things of spectacular interest
but I cannot say these things so you will understand them.
For to understand what I convey, you also must be insane,
always between the lines the silent language
of eyes and the many positions of the feet.
These stories, difficult to transmit using the vocabulary
I was taught to speak.

I am one of the crazy ones
my life is to jump and sing
I go into the market stalls
into the world of chicken cakes, live poultry,

I am one of the crazy ones
my love is to jump and sing
I go into the market stalls
push the dancing air before me
the poultry comes alive,
long robes cause a small dust.
You take me to the lake
slip into my shape and space
on the trail we gathered and ate dirt
together.
I am one of the crazy ones
our feet dance where we please
I take my music and mime on the tiles
of the Big Guy's courtyard.
I take dictation from
a long line of crazy ones.
You take me to the lake.

You sing, come O crazy one, come with me
to the lake, on the trail we lay
and ate dirt together.
I slip you on, you slip into me on the trail
and on the trail we meet others like ourselves,
we meet others like us
You take me to the lake

you sing, come O crazy one
and on the trail I slip you on, you slip into me
I am one with the crazy ones
our feet dance where we please
I take my music and mime tribal rhythms
on the tiles of the Big Guy's courtyard
I take dictation
from a long line of crazy ones.

PART ONE

Aeneas Was A Dreamer

I am Aeneas, the wanderer
a warrior who has lost his homeland
and now searches for a new place to plant my flag. My magic
bundle is a citadel where my home gods live. I am responsible for
their places at the table. I was ordained to carry the gods far
from our old world and so we built temples and sacred
gardens at various points in our journey.

We shall make a single Troy in spirit,
may this task be honored by our children.

Aeneas was a dreamer, Aeneas the Trojan warrior begins to wend
his way west, the smoke from the Greek fires as they burned Troy,
made breathing hard. There was room for a prayer between every
                    breath.
Poems wrote themselves at night in the form of dreams. Language
saves the forgotten. Inside Aeneas's head was a big balloon, let loose
at a small carnival near Rio and it flew inside his head.
It read
"How slowly we fade from view, the empty spots."

Aeneas was a dreamer. He said to his mother, the Sly One,
the Goddess of Laughter, "I've hunted for you for so long that I came
upon my own tracks, made years ago."

Aeneas's Opening Song

I am the stitcher of songs, a wandering performer from occasion to
occasion, hoping for payment of some kind, a room or a meal.

Our songs and stories are the stories of a horse people.
We travelled, saw territory, battled with some, married others
rode to the edge of the world and kept our God, Athena, She of the
blazing eye in honor, building shrines and sanctuary, for it was
Her fields that nourished our horses and hills.

Invisibility was our ally, memories, shadows and dreams. Using
these various tricks we escaped many perils. The wandering people
of Troy are optimistic and our stories will be determined by the
kind of people we are.

My song can induce even the stones to go with
me and aid passage over the streams.

It will stand that I had to be the schemer, allowing Loki
his due, tricks played, a sleight of hand. I knew things that would
             help us
navigate the distant seas, games will have to be played with other
             nations,
for we must move on certainly, our fate is to find and not to war, so
I must negotiate, I am known by the horsemen as the schemer.

My song is not a holy story that needs to be
repeated, recited ceremoniously at certain times
certain hours, day or night, for my song
is the poetry of combat language.

Mother, Did You Ring

The Birth

I became a man with no country, Mother, in that ghastly stillness of
        a frozen night,
when all bodies become adrift, and float like puffs of dark blossoms,
        I too floated off.
I was born in the crackly winter air and became a man with no
        country, just adrift, like
you, in the ghastly stillness.
And what is the shape of a man of no country, a man who cannot say,
        I knew these
cows, I knew their kin Bossie, I cannot say that the cows I knew have
        floated off also,
into the stars like all the bears before them, a cosmos of memory,
        floating puffs. A
town, Tyrone, a place of cows and blacksmiths, plough horses, like
        planets line up by
the fence, they are in alignment, old suns, old stars, old planets, they
        circulate, I'm
with them, I leave no shadow, there will be no nuclear mark, no
        etchings. The man
with no country can have no landing place. And so, Mother, if a man
        cannot be
defined by geography, he becomes a ghost, at one with things long
        long gone, no
longer able to count the sheep in the meadow, the cows in the corn,
        I've become the
untethered planet, a man with no country.
I thought it would be a lot easier, there are so many pictures of our
        clan on the
ground, there, me, by the fence, standing with the horse, and there's
        us, a whole row

of us, all with our heads stuck through a cardboard cut-out display of
unfaced

cowboys, at the Sarnia Fair that autumn. I get those pictures out once
in awhile,

cardboard cowboys, yippie yi oh, a mosquito was biting my ear as I
recall. Does this

not make me a man with a country, of course, the man is Remember,
the place

Together.

I thought it would be a lot easier, so much evidence of earth, but the
winter night has

brought a freeze into the blood, a naturalness now for the cold
hollow. We didn't

perish during the ice age, we learned some huddle, some ancient step,
a pounding

beat, a double tap on the downstroke, we climbed ice walls, forced
our way to the

edge of chasms, forged ice picks out of horn, worked towards the
north, digging, a

face to scale, and we cremated our dead on the pink rock of our
homeland.

A small bird told me you danced in the ancient manner, your veil fell
revealing your

shadowy self.

I danced as if dogs were yapping at my heels, get back, back, I kick
with strange

venom, get back. There are corrections to be made, a center of
balance, the forming

of a tight knot and so gymnastics came easily, a toss of gravity over
my shoulder, for

although I was afloat and I felt a knot, I began a sense of which
direction lay north.

How ghastly cold it is in outer space.

Using the words I know now, I wonder.

Always under these circumstances it's good to check veracity,
          Mother. Is this ethereal soup
that we're adrift in, is this perhaps a bad stage setting, cheesy tinsel,
          chintzy stars,
dust on platforms, and someone thought there was an animal act and
          brought some
jackass who's backstage complaining.

Is this your bad, empty theater deal, where they quit earlier, locked
          up and left off,
and in the dim, floating in the dust, little dust planets, puffs, you and
          me, adrift, in
the ghastly stillness of the bad stage play called a man with no
          country, Mother did
you ring?

***

The smell of ether was strong. I coughed,
a light came on, the heartbeat of the
motherland, the jungle drumming of a wild thing, I floated off,
began counting the rhythm of my own heart.

Canyon de Chelle

How sere the eyes that can see death coming.
My beloved ghost, you will die a second time with me.
That's where it starts in the continent of ghosts, with me reading
mother's heartbeat.
She was being called back to the sea, even as I was being torn from it.
The dreams of dolphins lapped against my eyelids in passage,
the Phantom Limbs, the armature of belief,
a continent of ghosts,
transference of
gene-power to the life within.

You gave me enlarged breath to power the heart, an extended
            breath, the high crazy note to shade the
day. I have come to channel the ancient information, taken off the
            walls of your birth canal. Stick
drawings, the horse, five lives by a river, plumes seemed to be in the
            style. Old pictures on the walls of
your canyon, I want to camp out but I must hurry.
To slumber, slump against your canyon wall, press my nose gently,
            take in your flavor, every orifice is
awake, there are dreams, streaming out through my tear ducts, I see
            my last view, the first view lies ahead,
out of the canyon of the lost child, light, ahead, birds pass before the
            opening, geese, only later did I know
of this, at the lake one time, at dusk, the geese of my earliest memory
            returned, in formation, a dashing,
sink to the lake surface, and stillness in my dream. With my cheek
            pressed against your canyon wall,
Mother, I saw geese, later I thought, how well you prepared me for
            how alert I would have to be without you.
She had a ferocious heart, her talons of genetic power pierced me.

Her teeth knew how to guide the unwary onto the path of death, where
          long limbs of genetic power
dangle, able to darken the light from above, the canopy on the path of
          death is thick and the unwary may
lose their way.
She went to all the old magic spots, but death had kicked in the two
          doors where entry was certain, no
magic, no secret location protected by berry vines and no trick step,
          no one-nostril breather, it was, finally
an end of places of magic, and so, what earthly reason is there in
          staying? When you bit the umbilical cord
and set me free, you left shortly thereafter yourself.

I heard your voice once, Mother, it came up out of the alder trees
          disguised as a wind. Like a yodel it
came and shrieked, I cannot make you immortal, you will die
          someday when your number comes up, but
I can protect you as only a mother can, for I am Aphrodite and you
          are my son who will forever bear the
burden of his father.
Every time I touch you
              it is a signal that I am leaving
              bury me with our dancing ancestors
              the skull and antler people.

She's wandered off, into her own hunting dream now,
as if the taste of blood could reveal a new story she could join
and begin anew. So it shall be with myself too, a wanderer
in a dream, you are ahead, I hunt, I need blood, but I hadn't realized
it would be so formal as to meet you in death.

I was left unfinished, the early birth, dropped off on
a backwater highway near a concrete warehouse with a truck ramp.
There was sun or at least bright light, and it seemed to be
warmer, but isn't that the way of it when you just come out of
the water. It wasn't my time yet and I was arriving now, unfinished.
It was a rural town, I heard the chickens out back. Two lost their
        heads over
the birth of a boy. I arrived my face not fully closed,
a cleft in the palette, not fully closed, I arrived. It was a rural
town in the north. They had chickens. Later I found out there were
two cows in the barn.
I arrived unfinished, not formed to perfection and it had a
profound effect on who I became. You left shortly thereafter, 'hoisted'
        as
Leonard so sadly said.
I didn't notice your absence, I was left unfinished, I was making a
        plan. Later, I
began to suspect there was something just outside the frame.
The breath of my mother in this moment contained all the
wisdom that I will ever need. I was born smarter than I will
ever be again. I had the air of water, gill-faced air and warmth
from the flood of light, this gill-faced air, full of stories,
picture stick figures, holy breath. We shared.
All this was present that night on this stranger's farm.

When we are in mortal danger, we run, like bears do, to a tree, the
        tree where
man was born, where we have always been safe, invisible to our
        enemies, only

to die when the dogs come, and so it was, I was in a tree when the
        dogs came
and I died out of that world and into this one, early, not quite finished,
        but
danger had led me to a tree and I heard the dogs coming in the
        distance.

My Time Is The Den Of The Magician

Mother, in my language, we called you home.
I sense you amongst the shadows, I look for your shape
there, in the small leaves around my tent. It looks like a cat's
head, ears perked as if listening, for what, footfalls on the canoe
dock. At night someone has come ashore from the dark lake, is it
me, dark one, for which you dream?
My time is the den of the magician, in partnership, we are two
tangoists, you hate the dirty bastards that smoke, you say in my
ear, "those bastards smoke and stare at my crotch."
Hold on, I enjoy the boyish cut that you have adopted, your
cockeyed evil eye.
How could the sun always be crescent in your world, is this the red
world from which you came and went, is this the piercing red world
from which you came to me, saying, welcome to the red world, fire
will be your friend and I will set you on fire many times and the
last fire will be the final fire.

The Burning of Troy

And there will be holocaust. A great fire will take out a great
city. This city will be called Troy, and with this fire
all deals are up for grabs. All news new, all shadows
still, all hearts rent, all up for grabs, art, music, poetry. It was
to start anew, all questions had to be re-asked, all answers
reinvested with the power of mythology. Start with the bone
suckle of its marrow. There will be steadying steps, though tiny,
and we must take it to foreign shores.

There will be a holocaust. A great fire will take out a whole
population. You can find a tableau, behind a fence, a yard that
had washing, an apron and a butterfly are forever etched
in concrete. Cats went, caged birds,
a whole population. The ignominy of it sucked away,
flashed to the bone, destroyed forever mythology
of a certain kind and a certain history. Gone with the light of jihad
reckoning. Music and poetry and culture frozen, etched like
aprons and butterflies.

There will be a holocaust. Men of martial will, small boys
doing their master's bidding
with the light of jihad's reckoning.
In quiet places there are men not afraid of holocaust. They know
only that for a while, no small birds came
from the south. There was no migration from the south, no long
trails in the sky, no fingers of long birdlife, wandering
and gathering their forces, their long wedge formations,
against a first quarter moon.
In quiet places men noted some screeching metallic disturbances
some siren parting of the night air, some flashing orange
fire, a color captured later and reinvented as
the color of masks worn on certain nights during the month of

August, this orange color was noted. At sunset they would gather
on this mountain, from whose side you can see the roof of the
world. These quiet men circled, danced, became frenzied,
fell and were still, remembering nothing. They were wise.
Red wine will make you sick, spinning will make you forget.

There will be holocaust, great fire, systems under attack. There'll
be reinvention, white-faced cattle mimes, black-face sheep tragedians.
Here there used to be hundreds of acres of green grass
worked over by mimes and tragedians, circus of towns and villages,
interconnected, lifelines, like bird lines, wandering and gathering
            forces.
Fire took them out.

There will be holocaust, erasure by fire. Parchment with the old story,
crumpled, distended, blown apart, many sections carried
by many winds, each with the sad responsibility. The old songs!
The humming of a thousand voices, in a valley, near the big forest,
the old songs, the humming, evening, a thousand voices rising as
one voice, till dark, and a thousand candles
flickered on, buffeted by a wind that makes you sad for no known
            reason.
There'll be hands on fire and eyes on fire and vision on red, and red
on lips and fire on red and story on fire. We were married
in red. I was in red. You, too. In war it is red. I will go to it.
There will be hands on fire, and ribbons where eyes used to be.

There will be silence after holocaust, for a long time. Holocaust,
death by predetermination, then silence.
We are the mute, like cattle, stooped to the black earth.
Grass may begin to grow here. A green snake may come, some
arteries, some grass, some green, many shades, may come here
and a stream and a fish dropped by a bird. It may all come here again.

The most severe penalty for being the son of a god was she would
          never let you
fall in love. She was jealous in the extreme and although we visited
          many ports
where strangers called out, "Give me something that will be carried
          away by the
wind," I did not go ashore. My mother was like that.
She could not make me immortal, in vain were her efforts, I would
          finish my
mortal coil at the appropriate time, decided by forces where stray cats
          roam the streets,
but she could, and did, snatch me away from death 8 times, and 8
          being
the royal number of death, I thought it would behoove me to get on
          with my
story, the journey across the seas of my life span, the odyssey.
And so it is to the Holy Ghost that I turn first. Eventually, you get to
          live with
the fact that you will never be allowed to fall in love, that package
          was denied
delivery. "I think you want the guy next door," I would point out.
          Well actually,
mother spoke, using me as her megaphone. I was always answering
          questions with
answers that baffle me. And then she said, "I will always give you the
things that you will need to prosper. You will always dance the
          tango, at late
hours, you will gamble with an empty heart, I will infest you with
          Loki, the

trickster from the north, you will see around things, visit penthouses
        in New

York and wildcat buildings in the Lower Eastside, where large men
        guard the door.

You will travel with paper sacks and warm cups of coffee. All this
        and much

more I will help you to traverse. I only ask one thing: you will
        always, forever

always be loyal to me, Aphrodite. I am the Mother and you are the
        son. There

will only be room for one on the edge where you will be forced to
        travel."

I knew then what her price would be.

This travel, this journey business, when did it all start? Right after
        the disaster

where you, Mother, announced to me, that you were the royal We
        and you have

been summoned home, to the mountains.

PART TWO

Stories The Waters Tell

Aeneas Hypnotizes Himself

In order to fall asleep at night, I invent whole landscapes in my mind. I hypnotize myself with the details of the pre-sleep world, ever growing in dimension as I get older. I call it The Stories That The Waters Tell.

The stories that the waters tell are the stories about those lost in the Urge, to lean forward, forced to wander, seeking what, some mythical pathway to yesterdays' adventures. The Urge, it gnaws at me, the Wanderer. It's the wrong time and the wrong place, but it's your place and it's a lovely place to me. Songs we hum along the trail to fill in the empty space where you used to be, the Wanderer fills his head with rosy stories, pink sunsets, but apart from you, my dear, I am joined on the trail by my shadow, Belial, agent of Satan. He shows me how to skim the edge, to pick from nothing its very heart. I must press on, I must press upon the moment of my life with someone else, a small boy peeking from behind a granite landscape, rocks of every size and dimension, obstacles, in-your-face threats.

In this landscape of the Underworld of sleep, my song beckons the stones to follow me and aid in my passing over streams and the stories waters tell. I go to this underworld to search for my father, Anchises, for I have a question: "Where has my darling young one gone?" Questions I ask myself at night as I lay in my cocoon of bear smells and memories. I recall another time. There were many lost people on the move. I was one of them.

My pathway to sleep leads to our capital city of Ras Sharma, a thriving metropolis that moves from place to place and follows like a faithful dog. I will take you for a moment into the land of the Urge people, you will meet my father, Anchises, and my shadow, Belial, who promised me, the Wanderer, all glory if only I would forget my song of loyalty to my mother, calling to her in our ancient tongue. Uhuru,
Plant your flag, I will come.

The Urge To Lean Forward With Expectation

Inside the peninsula of the Urge you have a whole living world
made of magic and mythology, a narrow landscape on whose fires
the pot is always boiling.

I was born with Saint Vitus' dance, an uncontrollable twitch at the
shadow line, the edge of things, fire and ice, the heat to gamble,
the ice to deny interference.

The moon is shaped like a gun,
the hunting instinct is so dangerous it has to be chained at night.
The headwaters of the elephant's path, the travels home.
The urge to roll in our dead
for even in the breasts of sparrows, the drums of Odin roll,
there are some eyes that are not empty.

I knew I was screwing up even as I tried to please the cloud-people,
agents for Belial, accomplice of Satan. Belial represented the
Urge, and he had infected me early. Girls and racehorses, much
                    sadness,
many got hurt in my early flights to my invented world.
The Urge grows, each day a little bird comes with stories and
a few feathers grow overnight. You don't notice that
this odd bird is growing until one day you realize that your
bird has told you nothing but bad stories dictated from the heart of
                    Belial,
"Take it, it is going to be easy."
Your bird has become a black raven and scours the hillsides for dead
                    sheep,
looking for something for nothing, always a predator, alert for any
rustling in the bushes. That was me, the Urge, press forward
                    regardless
of the consequences. I would gamble the rent money.

Belial is the shape of all the evil things you've done,
a real presence, a density you can not see but an instinct tells
us there is someone beside you, holding open scissors.

Belial (Satan's Envoy)

Belial's eyes were the color of amber, irregular shapes with
the skeletons of small creatures trapped inside. Black thoughts
lurked in the corners like foxes.
Belial looked at you from a distance so far back in his head that
the sky was darkened by ravens, black defenders who whirl.
In the far, far background were turreted ice-palaces of indifference
as if on the ebb-tide of life, sequences were carried out over the sea
in a convex pattern, like a roomful of dervishes, memorized.

Belial could see far highways in your eyes, paths to the soul.
It would be on desperate roads where we meet, in auto graveyards,
a geometry of stick-angles and glossy oil. He'll glance at you
through passing sticks.
And when Belial speaks to me, I hear calypso music, downtown is
happening, guys are crying the blues, women are eating it up.
All the accursed are beautiful, as if a thin edge of their lives, with its
              craving
ability uncovers creatures that can pass through boundaries like a mist,
reappearing with an irascible sparkle
like monkey-gold dust,
an illusion that you can get something for nothing, but precise,
where the trust level is renewed every day.

O, my trusted brother, my twin, you in the deep shadows, revealed
only in oily water, a glimpse through the junkyards, you pass
down the aisles of rusted, damaged, metal shards, each honed to a
different level of death.

Belial, famed in mystical tales from India, the darkest of continents
where the children of the poor eat the children of the poor.
Belial was beautiful and when he looked upon you, he thought,
go away and die in your little world.

Belial, Like A Second Skin, He Follows Me

He revealed himself, some odd stick-angles.
In his face, the valleys were sunless
not black, not brown, sunless
so, to approach, you found yourself in shaded light
it was his way and it had been handed down.

He revealed himself, a fetish,
some junky string, some Chinese mirrors
bits of ribbon, silvery
as if
we have death at nine-fifteen
it was his way and it had been handed down.
He revealed himself, saddle-pump shoes,
a yellow tie
a stepout outfit that inhabits space
as if
time alone needs a harness partner.

It was his way and it had been handed down
to lump and crunch was not enough,
to lump and crunch and roll on was not enough
to watch out for dog shit on the floor
was not enough.
Awake at odd angles was enough.
It was his way and it had been handed down.
This is not going to be fun necessarily, but where is
my little darling, marching down the hill like…
He revealed himself as notes, played against the melody line
harsh, little yodels, whistles at a distance through fog,
pounding with wooden sticks, as if to put an ear to his own voice
deepen the reverb,
begin to work in new tunes, over his own voice.
It was his way and it had been handed down, a high harmony
it was his way and it had been handed down.

Ras Sharma: The City of My Dreams

Each night a city of 800 tents and huts sprang up in an instant. Each
        day
skirmishing parties of warriors replenished supplies by pillaging
and despoiling the wayside villages.
We moved always in the path of the wind. To be free of bugs was to
        be free
from cholera. The trail behind was littered by bodies.
Sometimes there was such a great sadness of miming. Theater got so
multidimensional that the capital Ras Sharma would sit still for
        months.
Real life was portrayed in weird little street dramas. A group of
        players,
an awning, everywhere, up and down every street you could stand and
watch, join in or watch yourself watch you.
Great Actors had careers that lasted weeks.

There were problems with moving our Capital from place to place.
        The
Grand Tents sat on hills, for the breeze. But the tents of the clerks, tax
collectors, officers of the Guard, these were in the suburbs, mid the
        dips,
breathless and dry. The Rabble parked where they could and drank
        Rah, a
fermented fruit. The Capital was moved when the cockfights
        degenerated
into brawling rebellion. The Mighty Red Tents were packed onto
        camels
and we moved on.

The Light At Night

There had been a great fire in the hills before we arrived ... I could
> tell, the trees were
like lonely monuments, like tired soldiers, a respectful distance
> between each, the
way it is with tired men. The trees were snow-covered now, the
> hillsides were
undecided now, some white, some where black powder shone
> through.

Far in the background there were drums
and behind that, a tin whistle flute.
I couldn't see much
the hills
occasionally lit by jumping fire
were in the way.
The tin flute seemed solitary.
There was much evidence of industry.
The wild things headed out
at their pace,
toward the leaping hills
and the red fire at night.
My life is stretched out along the ghost migration.

We did bundle our souls for the journey. Many took refuge in cruel forms of humor. The practical joke, the pie in the face at a funeral, sorry to see the loved one pass on, splat! Many found this stuff funny. If we camped for longer than a week at any one place, whole Carny groups formed. Individual anarchy reigned. Six guys were working the fringes as Eva Peron. Singers sang the gossip aloud wherever three tents met. The constant milling, the constant dust, were theatre stages, to step into and out of until one forgot whether it was Entry or Exit.

Normally we burned the dead. It was too tough to dig a hole. We'd make a big pile of buffalo chips, lay the loved one down carefully, light the thing and move back upwind. A little altar was built, really just a few stones piled up, but the flowers were fresh. Some words were said, each of us to our special darkness, each welcoming the spirit, open to aid the confusion that must be present. Afterwards, some were drunk and some were singed from being too close to the fire. Mounting up to ride off was difficult for the drunks and painful for the singed.

Oh, we did sing strange songs to our children in the evenings. Fire sparks sweep skyward into the darkness. We trebled our vicious hymns, harmonies reaching through the night, gathering force at each campfire. We sang strange songs to our children. The various twangs, different locations, the north, the eastern tribes, gatekeepers for the sun. Songbirds need to hear their own songs sung back to them by others of their species. You can lose your song if you do not mingle with those of your own kind. We sang our songs at night around the fires, we'd hum our kids to sleep. We sang the old tunes from far across history, old wars, great battles, horses of renown. Sappho led the singing many nights. Bridal songs to the richest man in town.

When Joshua died, the horn section was tremendous. Music was made
late into the night, in small clubs, down alleys. People sat quiet
in the red glow of cigarettes.

On a flat mesa near the city gathered the African choir playing long
            hollow
kelp horns, the horns of the sea. Joshua overcame many kings. He'd
unlimber, cummerbund red, play a note so unruly concrete owls were
knocked completely over.
The eastern tribes returned home. For six days the harelips arrived.
            Ponies
draped in scalps and black raven feathers. At night drunken arm
wrestling broke out. Their campfires dotted the hills, fiery violent
            places
of streaming sparks. Whole trees were set on fire, arrows honed for
the heartkill. The musician's union held a benefit at the Crown Hall.
Barney Fenders' Top Hats played for minimum. An
expensive red wine was served. Joshua's farewell was well attended.

It sure was dusty in Egypt. On everything. The false choppers.
Once a week a guy came with a cart and gathered up everybody
        who'd coughed to death.
Mistress Antoine of the Veil saw no decline in business in her line
        of work.
She actually enjoyed exposing clever little deceits. Her brother Iliad
        the
Fancier bought land cheap next to a dry riverbed. When it finally
        rained all his goods
got washed away by prosperity.
It was near the end of the beginning that we realized that the seats
        were merely rented.

The March At Midnight

We came down the hill toward this city after dark. Miles of us, the wanderers infused with the power of the hunt. When the last group could see the city glowing before us, we stopped. There were stars but no moon, just a city, throbbing with life, as colored light flashed high and low, like water rippling off certain rocks. One could hear dogs barking, but we stood still, remembering when we had a city and danced late at night. The wind was non-directional, but swirling like personal histories that constantly slap the face.

We were going to move on, our place was not here in the land of the Urnfield people, those who bury their dead in pots they leave by the roadside. We have come across these urns many times. Fresh flowers are scattered and we just move on.

And there was one who did run for it and we turned and watched her, a mighty rustling did rent the air, yet no one moved to help her. She was making it, it was a long hill up to the city of lights, she's almost there. But they turned the lights out. She was in a big darkness. The air became still, we moved off. I thought I'd have a drawing made of the kids.

Tecumseh the Orator had a brother, the Prophet. This prophet did
            tell the
gathering of all the peoples,
"Although the honkies are as many as the leaves on the trees
they will not conquer our hearts. I see a man, Red Cloud, and his
people, the so few, in the snow on the mountains, and they are lost.
            The Lord
Harry does watch them, but they are sore and in need. I, the Prophet
            do beseech
you to send a prayer for a future man named Red Cloud, alone with
            his brothers,
damp faces reading the wind."

.

RED CLOUD: *Today I wondered*

The Law Of The Small Clan

We were few
one had to go
so the rest could live, she said.

***

My heart will never heal for the loss of the Old Ones.
To leave the Old Ones on the trail behind us, in the snow,
yet we must move on. The sky and the small birds warn of more
snow and our enemy is just behind the wind, riding.
As we move off, each knowing that for the rest of us to survive we
                must migrate
north to safety. I walk with my eyes lowered.
I think of the Old Ones, propped up, facing the eastern gate,
                knowing the sun will
come up again and again and then you go to sleep to freeze and
                mummify into snow-
frozen holy places, where a soul once lived, but we must move on,
                and leave
our enemy lost amid the magic of our old holy ones, snow-covered
                mounds.
And so it was with you...
I left you on the trail
a pillar of snow
a soul of a soul
waiting to be reborn.

Rooting Around With The Ancestors Of the Cree

Armageddon would be a step up for us.

I travelled with a cat, and while chopping the wood for one of the
many campfires, I keep an eye out for the safety of the cat. It was a
lesson, be able to handle two serious thoughts at the same time. I
was trying to figure that out whilst in the bloody boonies, Troy
smoking in ruins behind us, it was the open road. The cat joined me
early on, I needed someone to do battle with. After all, there was the
gap, all the adrenalin shot. The Greeks packed up the klieg lights,
turned off the water taps, set a bunch of fires, and here I am. The cat
Coboss is my partner. I need to foster the ability to have two
thoughts at the same time. I expect no help from a cat whose name
translates to Come Hither Cow. Rooting around with the ancestors
of the Crees.

Uphill, downhill, across streams, through bogs and mires, I follow
something I hope leads me back to my father's land, for it is there
that I will see the beginning, be able to look beyond the present into
the para-reality of hallucination. They say you go around twice. I
will pass Go, collect two hundred dollars of fake money and start
over, always with the wish to land on Park Place. Aeneas remembered
when he had a doorman. A guy who called out at his beckoning,
"Carriage for Mr. Aeneas."

Periodically, the cat would run out of gas, need to lay down,
stretch and stare into space. And there had been a lot of nippin' about,
and to what avail. That is what Coboss thought. How cum we just
            don't camp
here, there's a wishing well, the scrubbery seems alive with mice,
something might come along.

I thought about this particular idea, that something might come along.
We don't have to worry about those bastards from Greece,
by the time they will have finished with setting fires, I will
have moved on to another dimension.

I'm suffering from post-war syndrome, regular old life just seems
          very flat.
I mean flat, sucked free of air flat, imploded to an even temperature
flat. I mean I'm wandering around among seriously dangerous
          savages,
with a cat. That I'm keeping an eye out for. Two ideas at the same
          time.
Our story now begins.

As I've said before, Aeneas travelled with a cat who just seemed to follow him, resting when he did, and catching varmints when he was at war. And here was his father dying, the sadness that comes to the human heart when one recognizes that the end is near for a loved one.

But Aphrodite, the mother, the God of Sly Looks, had provided Aeneas with a sacred bundle, and in his sacred bundle, Aeneas wrapped his father up and carried him on his back until Anchises' flame flickered out and Aeneas again took up his sacred bundle and, followed by a coon-like cat, he issued orders.

Try to keep up. We are looking for a new place to start over. We will build new cities, but we will wander, always asking advice from the cruel winds. Take heart, the Gods of Ilium travel with us, and as long as we live, they too shall live. Bring your clay pots, your dogs that can search for water, carry the children over the huge rocks.

The small birds bring me the news that the mighty Odysseus, known as the man of tactics, has headed for his home to his wife. His journey goes in fits and starts. He weeps, his heart drained of adrenalin, the enlightened air of warfare. I hear the mighty Odysseus is sad, whereas, we who lost our wives to slavery, saw our children hurled from the walls, who saw warrior-fathers carried home on their shields, we the lost wanderers, guided and protected by the Goddess of Laughter, we celebrate the new day, wash our horses gladly at the flowing waters, we move to our fate, and sing aloud our yodel-song as we move towards nightfall. At this point, experience itself is the object. We travel towards the Happy Isles, the Elysian Fields.

All this we can do. I know in my heart that the Greeks, they too wander. The mighty Odysseus, he will face many harms for the burning of Ilium. He goes home to the flat lands and we go to the seven hills of forever.

Two People Sharing One Tragedy
Aeneas The Warrior

I sent my armies into the field. First went the peacocks, with
ribbons flying. The sun did not bother them.

On June the twenty-first there was a blue moon, killing all
the herons on the upper Fraser River Valley. It was then I
released the second wave, cheetahs.

Cheetahs ranged over the field. Their claws were dipped
in rattlesnake blood. There was no sun in
the place of the cheetah.

Ponderous beasts came next, ending the agony of the wounded.

Birds were swept from the skies by winds that
threatened the presence of the moon. Beasts rumbled to
semi-life on the oceans' bottoms. Hulks that covered miles
of the sea floor struggled for a thought.
At one point a string of bountiful oases lay in our path.
Huge palm trees swayed in the glow cast up from the deep
waters. Breezes darted and birds of royal colors sang in the
trees. The peacocks stripped the trees and fouled the water.
The cheetahs raked everything that moved and ponderous
beasts flattened the earth.

To say that I am sorry does not seem like enough.
There is darkness in places of the heart in transit.

Periodically, We Need to Account for Ourselves

I always face a parade of cloud-gods, ring-tailed snorters
when I am alone in the sky-kingdom.
In anger the cloud-gods speak to me of war.
"With each tree lost, we lose any chance
for a three-dimensional existence.
The horizon at sunset will become a long alligator.
On the alligator's back ancient cities will rise."

Coventina, The Nymph Who Presides

They said she could reappear at will
the pretty girl
who walks to town
across the meadows,
hopping the stone fence
at the miller's bend.

Bright yellow are her ribbons this spring day.
After a sunshower, she goes to town
crossing the slick green meadows
where the black bulls feed.

She darts along the stone fence
nimbly over the jagged owl's nest
and drops beside my listening post
by the watering trough.
She is curious about which fine men have passed.
The pretty girl could reappear at will
she could go by, then go by again.

There were many ribbons, some yellow
and chevaliers, flamboyant parties of men
bedecked with fancy medals and peacock feathers.
Riotous laughing produced from the air riotous colors
as a jumble, dust kicked up by the horses
and cloaks, long and sweeping the ground.

I'm stuck here with my responsibility of recording.
They've all disappeared into town.

Now she is approaching on foot, I see her in the dusk.
She's at sunset tonight and the reds, yellows

melt into the rainwater puddles
trapped for awhile
even after the sun has set.
She comes stepping through
these last puddles of sunset
ambers and purples flush through her toes.
She gives me a wink
this pretty girl
and climbs the stone fence
and climbs the stone fence.

Evening

Aeneas stood in the makeshift corral with his back to the
barn. A grey April evening is drifting in over the valley
bringing with it the low clouds and spattering rain that the
man expected. He stood very still and listened to the birds
as they closed out the day. The man looked around him very slowly
at the low cast sky, at the fields, mottled snow, white and
green, and at the rustling spring forest. He looked at the horse,
still now at day's end and he thought on how her front feet
needed clipping. The winter's wood lay at skelters about the
corral, skinny, fragile sticks, abandoned now, yet these were
the same ones he had dug through the winter snow to retrieve.
Aeneas no longer needed them and he did not see them. Nor did
he see the dogs, but the smell of skunk hung in his nostrils
and he knew they were close behind him. The man stood,
leaned on the corral fence, and hummed a tune from the old country
glorifying the men lost at war, his old pal
the mighty Phyleus, known as the alligator.

Aeneas Confers With The Birds

When Aeneas is not contemplating the horses,
he is a bird watcher, for in a dream, his mother came to him
            disguised
as a black swan and said to Aeneas, I am the mother of illusion,
I am both black and white. I will send messages to you using the
            small
birds and you will see them as good fortune, the bearers
of welcome news.

Aeneas would sit outside his cabin even in the storms of
            midwinter.
He would sit under the trees and watch the small birds
cavort among the alders. The little banditos, he called them.
Birds are oracles of the future. Every army had a bird-reader, a
designated listener to the stories small birds tell. His sole task
was to interpret what gossips the birds were exchanging.
Aeneas kept this man close and paid attention.

I watch the wind come through the water trees on tiny feet. Leaf by leaf it approaches, fresh off the river, just in from the sea, tiny steps now, no longer the fear of a watery death, the wind glides home, lands leaf by leaf at my window, and now the wind is perched around the cabin, I hear strange news in foreign trills. The wind has come from Asia, it smells of wild horses. It smells of death to me. Ponies with bits of raw scalp plastered to their neck. The wind brings serious news. Wind chimes alert me to change in tone.

I watch the wind come in on tiny feet, shaking up the leaves, all the wild birds. It could be the news, it could be the news, but only fog seems evident, the wind has taken a form, the wild birds dart about in the belly of the wind. The fog is making me seasick, *mal de mer,* of lunar influence. I couldn't disagree with that.

I entered the age of befuddlement
by enjoying the ballet of the birds
performed in the alder trees
by the cabin, the ensemble
cachet de poulon grande
the piece,
the elephant walk to their homeland.
The leaves are gone
blew off by the heavy wind,
leaves and wind disappeared down the roadway
and now the ensemble, the corps, if you will
are exercising, and stretching
leg over the bar
preparing to activate
when the band begins
they too wait for the high note
C above C.
The age of befuddlement begins
when all things become clustered together
have the same meaning, the same weight,
no distinction is necessary or wanted.
The ballet of the birds begins with a mass
of many high tunes, still in the bare branches,
leaves with slow breath, hollow limbs,
sugar rises with the cold and sun,
the note has been sent,
the heavy wind informs
the corps,
"a dash to stations, please."

Big Wind Makes The Wild Things Fly

The wind
with wild geese in fragments
coils the river.
Who was it said, the dead arrive full of themselves
having just gorged on memories.
Was it you
hopping around there on the other side of
See-Through-Me Creek.
The wind today brought five wild geese
far from their flyway.
Five are the cycles of life on a river.
Five interlocking circles, symbol of a river
interlocked, a horse, a drum, a yodel to call the cows
a mirror that reflects around corners.
The fifth sphere is a view of my last view of earth.
I have seen it once already. It comes around, like a water wheel
like a phase of the moon, first a sliver
then eclipse.

I feel the wind come up.
I'm alert to any slight breeze on my face. The light gets elongated
at the corner of my wild eye.
I remember my horse ancestors.

The wind is blowing the wild geese all over the place.
The wind blows the wild geese
in fragments they arrive
outward on the river.
The wind
with wild geese, in fragments,
coils.
Who was it that said the dead arrive full of themselves

having just gorged on their own memories.
Was it you,
hopping around there on the other side.
The wind today brought five wild geese in,
far from their flyway. Five like the circles of
life on a river. Five wild geese.

What is it you'll eternally do
in the last moment of life.
A sleigh ride dream, on a north face
the smell of wet wool.
I see you, a clown with a pet elephant,
you work small fairs, collect a fee
at the door, the pachyderm wraps its trunk
around your neck in the grand finale.
Dreams come in pairs, like socks
come in pairs, two the same shape,
almost a match, colorwise, this one though
has cable knitting, a conqueror's name,
a northern town
far from the sea,
an unusual drowning.
Dreams come in pairs, one flaps its soulwhite wings
the other dream, soul white itself, is still folded,
wing-work though clipped,
was still ahead. Like tame geese at a river,
wings knocked back, never sound sleep,
dreams, in pairs are behind your little back,
you see it once, and you know it will return,
first a sliver, then eclipse.
And that's the way of dreams, isn't it,
close order drill,
tight pachyderms, two for the price of one, Siamese singularities.

It is written in a black book that five is the end of things
on the mortal plane. It is the number of times you will resurface,
always stooped to a lawn chair, watching an ant run
across the white arm. Once it was a rocker.
In the melody in my head it runs five notes to the bar.

The other night the dog was scratching at the door, and just as
I was about to unlatch it, I realized the dog was already in.
Then who was outside pretending to be the dog. I said, in one
of my best falsettos, Is that you Belial, you
spider monkey man.
Turned out to be just leaves, swirling in the wind. How quickly,
I thought, do I call forth, again, the dubious but powerful theater
of the streets, the fake voice calling forth the God of Thunder,
the King of Jamboree. Finally, as he saw it, you just kept
singing, loudly, just bellow it out, like the
opera, hold the last note, a long note, a mantra
note, a yodel note, a five-beat-to-the-bar note,
a yodel that will call the cows.

Big wind makes the wild things fly,
makes the wild ancestors fly.
Big wind incites, electrically,
challenges the talons of respectability
to a tug of war,
seems to be thinking of something else
during your struggle with the damnedest.

The wind is the stroke of Jupiter,
if fire comes, invisible, the confidante of wind,
if anger, the paid companion of fire can be wrestled to a clearing
for execution,
then it's all still happening out there,
for the mirror that sees around corners is just perspective.
I've been given a short thread to unravel.

Aeneas Sees The Arc Of His Lifetime

Part One

"So we abode in the valley over against Beth-pe-or"

I see my landscape into a flatter view now, perhaps when the eyesight
        fades, three-
dimensionality is lost, but there seems to be less depth, the alder river
        trees, the sea
birds, the cats, all exist on one plane…
I feel like Moses, I've led my little army of thoughts, ideas, curses,
        Armageddons, ill
feeling, snarls and petrifications for over seventy years, led the
        charge uphill and
skulked away when the battle went against us and I was forced to plot
        up another
scheme that was going to save us all from the landlord. I feel like
        Moses, when he got
to the Promised Land, he wasn't going to be going over. The Lord
        Harry sayeth,
Take a seat lad, your kind, the bad skimmers, the Hoodoo smack-
        talkers *you*, your
lads will take a seat. The kids can go over, the bad boys and you go
        to the valley over
against the mountain, Beth-pe-or.
I see my landscape into a flatter view now.

Part Two

The Nature of the Journey Makes us Unfit for the Arrival

It was hard to realize our time had passed, I'd been leading this bunch
        for so long,

now the kids would cross the river and we would stay behind. With
        my associates,
we'll build a tent city here at the edge of the river where I can see
        'em. On
special days, maybe they'll bring the kids and relatives down to the
        shore and we'll
all wave across to each other, two major lion groups roaring at each
        other over the
chasm of time.

Maybe they'll bring the kids at first, and the grandkids. Of course
        none of them
know why the old boys and me need this and talk will develop for
        them to move on,
migrate further away, leave the river behind. I can see that. They'll
        be motivated by
the same things that moved us. We want to wrestle with the immediate
        god of the
instant. Room is required for that, lonely areas, great tundras, swamps,
        forests of
rock and moss.
It's funny to guide this orb, my life, so far, then have it flattened
        against the side of a
riverbank, giving me a kind of half-moon look, my beard is white, my
        hair is white, a
kind of half-moon look. When it rains I see myself in the streams
        when I drink.
Over here we're carting the boys off slowly. Every few days another
        coughs to death.

A Historical Note

In ancient times the household gods could become bored, strange fidgets were developed, a contest amongst the girls, who was the more beautiful, Juno, Goddess of Birth, She of the Light or Aphrodite, Goddess of Laughter and Love. The deciding opinion was to be made by Ares, the War God, and he chose Aphrodite. Juno was infuriated, vowed vengeance on Aphrodite's favorite child, Aeneas, and his father, Anchises, lover of Aphrodite.

Because of the mirror, mirror on the wall, Juno set in motion what was to become in real world time, the Punic Wars. Two royal cities, Carthage, where they worshiped Juno as Queen, and the city of Rome, which was the final destination of Aeneas and the city of love and laughter.

Juno: She of the Moira

She could see so clearly what empty was
how nothing occupied no space
how hollow a china cup could sound.
She saw so clearly.
And suddenly she broke out into her beautiful song,
her voice rising through the forest.
She called to the furies with her octave range, called forth cold
          plateaus
called forth lightning views of arid places,
with her power she sang steelworkers
off the sides of buildings.

Like a cat, Juno took down her lovers with one swipe of her paw for
no real reason, other than the smell of grease made her crazy. There
wasn't anything wrong with her eyesight, and, as she remarked to a
loitering Cybele as she hung up the wet washing, on a line strung
like a crossbow, "Tell me, O Seer, when I burn the ships and end the
dreams of the Wanderer, make him lose his familiar birdsong, will
he linger and forget in the arms of a princess, Dido, perhaps?"
Cybele was afraid to say what she knew must happen and yet she
knew that whatever power the gods had, they could not stop the
moon or impede the sun. Olympians could not do that, so she said,
"The Wanderer will remember his story and yodel it out so even the
lions in the hills know, Aeneas honors his mother."

Juno puts me in a trance and in this hypnotic state I see orchards.
She has moved me into an ethereal state where my mother can no
longer protect me. I see my mother as a human being, a girl running
in the orchards at night, in and out under the moonlit shadows, a
shadow herself, as there seems to be a tall bird waiting, to replace
her, a tall bird in the orchard at night, is my mother.

Juno

It was astonishing to her to find there was another side,
a different window, alien view
same kind of bird
of course, they were everywhere around the cabin, little darters
small swamp birds. She's
seen all kinds of small darters before,
but this was another side of things.
Vertigo, she said,
as she waited for the light to change.
On the other side of things, you were always dressed better,
calf-skin gloves that went to the elbow,
cashmere coats that tied at the waist,
and scarves. When she went out into the ordinary side of things
she shone. But this is a different angle, alien view,
another side of what, she wondered.

Aeneas Visits the Underworld

Anchises the Father's Advice to Aeneas, His Son

Aeneas, through the intervention of his mother, Aphrodite, goes to the Underworld to search for his father. Aeneas wants to know what is in the future. He asks his father,

"Father, you of the keen eye, lover of my mother Aphrodite, what is in store for us, for me. Will we find our new place? We follow the southern sky at night, but there are many of our countrymen and I must have a sure hand."

"As for you my son," Anchises answered, "when you are born you are old and you spend the rest of your life working backwards, getting younger and younger until, egad, there is stuff dribbling off your chin. What has happened here, you may ask, are there going to be a million escapes, buckets of salt tears, or, as you slowly crash into childhood near the end, is it going to be just you and the stuffed bear gliding off, the ice skating duo on the ice planet of Eternity."

Aeneas asks, "What will become of us, will we reach a new homeland, will our gods, wrapped in my sacred bundle, will the gods of Ilium exist beyond today?"

And Anchises, father of Aeneas, answered thusly,
"Men have their appointments, moira, according
to which they must encounter a certain amount
of evil and misfortune, that fatal moment where
the gods will decide if you will live or perish.
We all carry a small package of lost. Do not
lose faith in the gold of the heart though there
may be times between glimmers. You won't know
what's missing until you know what's there.
A veil will be whipped away from your eyes. A window blind will
snap up, and before you lays a world of green-screen 3-dimensionality.
You will now dictate the tones.
The sky is not falling,
it's just another shade of blue.

Anchises the Father

As he passed under the Arches of Old Age, Anchises began to look
younger and younger, the various faces peeled back, exposing a
different shade of orange or black. Each year he lost weight, looked
   fit,
then one sunny morning Anchises emerged as a butterfly, did
antics in the sunlight.
Anchises was now beyond the cruel talons of Juno, she of the tribe
of Belial. She said, as she hung the wet laundry on the line in the
courtyard of Mount Olympus, It seems Aeneas's father has
   disappeared,
but she couldn't take her eye off a butterfly doing antics over her
   head.
And like any large predator, Juno became angry when something she
   wanted
escaped her. A blood moon rose somewhere over a walled city .

PART THREE

A Trick Of The Wind

I stayed behind in that barnyard memory
watching the old chickens, the half-blind dog
the axe embedded.
I saw you coming
kicking up dust
much like a Bedouin signals a friend
a fine spray of sand announced your arrival.

The yoke, the two, the pair
and is the yoke made of bone,
can it bruise, be brittle,
can calcium be the answer, mother's milk?
One by one, as the sun fell on us
we became animated.
And when your soul, fatigued by the passage,
made faint by the light, descends
to orange orchards in blossom,
orchards in the souls of wild things,
all animals have become you.
I stroke your shoulders
I think it helps
to calm you
my wild thing.

1

Shall we begin, you and I,
to follow the track of previous wanderers
into the stars
the final and last migration, the end
of staggery steps
and lost small animals
noted by the vacancy where the wind-wild wind
stirs in the dust circles,
I escape for a moment to warmer climes.

2

Don't ask me
to name the place from whence we come
nor the nature of the cloudless sky before us,
I will only feel the pressure of your hand in mine
as we join the chain of then and now.

3

It was through singing, as I recall
that we discovered our odd duet. Unsure of the language
I mimed your gestures
one day, before the oval mirror with the
stained glass border. There in the prisms,
I saw your image.
It was through singing that we formed our odd duet
one voice invisible.

Mother, You Are Above the Treetops

My first memory of learning about your death, I was three years old,
        in knee-pants.
Grandma was standing in the hallway by the kitchen, in silhouette,
        and she said,
"your mother has gone to the sky."
My next memory, I was on my swing under the apple tree and I
        looked across the
dirt road, and I saw the sky was very blue and seemed to be close. It
        was just above
the elm tree by the parsonage gate.
I thought, I will go and see the sky, then I will see you, Mother.
Country roads are dusty and I stood in the swirling and realized that
        you are
above the trees.

I looked up. I saw the sky through the branches and a cloud that
        seemed
itself snared, but I saw no mother trapped, no nest with a peeking
        owl, just blue
sky and clouds. I walked back. Soon I quit going, there wouldn't be
any rescuing involving that tree.

You became my bridge to strange things,
ghosts, filaments of
silver memory.
You have become a vessel to strange ports
to aim me
at distant shallows
where long-neck green birds live.

You became a river
starting in my youth,
running through long-legged lakes
life, accompanied by floating leaves, deep blue cedar forests,
we nested in the parting waters, the Ilando,
the place between winds,
in the silence where the mind no longer chatters.
I wait for us to travel to the shore
where they feel no need to blab the story.
Where, trapped in long silent lashes
near the eyes, in the eyes, a look
a transference, a story, trapped
near the eye, you became a river
you became a bridge, you became a vessel.

Try to write the story straight, would you. So much distance
between the words that I lose the thread, was it the cows were
coming or was it some girl, a girl from the orchards by the
look of her. I speak of these orchard girls in wild terms, in the
spring, when the orchards are heavy with blossoms, at night-time
     these
girls run together like wild horses, orchard girls behind a snorting
wind. I thought of you today, orchard girl.

Memories are like bird shadows, they flit for a moment.
I think your sweater was red
or was that another girl on the arctic steamboat.
The air, chilled by the ice floes
permeated us and we
had to return to your cabin.
You wore a red sweater.
I was known then, as Grey-eye

Mother, I dream of you once in a while
    this morning you were a decision where I was
        denying that I cared for this pile of stones.

***

We visited each other, small ships visiting foreign harbors. We sailed
in and out of each other's lives, brass bands would greet us at
canoe docks on remote Ontario lakes, the maples afire in the
autumnal silence across the lake, the wind down, a paddler's dream.
How vivid our colors melded, at this distance through time.
The rhythm of memories is the rhythm of breath while you were
in the womb, a gentle sway
the breath of life now in captivity
the kingdom of concerts, cherished by the old.
I hold the door open for the cat to come in
she brings with her garbled messages.

It was a mysterious kind of dance when we met. You said you were
        guided through the
steps by my fingertips. I moved and you could feel me.
"Here, put your hand, can't you feel him," you said. "He'll have
St. Vitus dance, I'm sure of it."
It wasn't an unhappy dance in the least. I could look into your eyes, of
        course, but as I've
said before, the jiggery steps made me laugh, and in my sleep I
        sometimes recall the
moment we laughed together. In the daylight hours I have no such
        dreams, but I do
practice the dance, in case I hear the band play.

Must I be rustproof
for you to love me,
must I go clank, clank into your heart.

The place where I am going in the end
is no longer there,
and yet, I stumble onward,
there could be a ghost
amongst the straw bales
or by the hay rick.
It could be you
one who was closest.
I swing out from the
barn's rafters
into the loose hay
waving towards me,
yet in the future,
and you
even then, in the past.

I Saw You Last

I am reminded of the way the wind was yesterday
by the way you flung your skirt
when you turned our corner.
The wind froze everything yesterday
like a lost galosh, still, black, with its metal dangling.

my birth, that is

I thought you were coming back, but it was a trick of the wind,
I think. The roar of your full-throated passing seemed to be going,
then, it seemed to be coming back, towards me, in my direction,
then, it was definitely moving away, to the north, your passing
joining the migratory flight paths and I knew your passing was over,
the sky was empty,
perhaps my birth was just a trick of the wind.

Running Water, Frozen Solid,
Still Stone

I'm not opposed to meeting you by the rocks,
hooded as they are by the drifted snow,
it could be like that other time
at Lake She-Be-She-Gone.
Winter is not the best time to be thinking
about separation,
at the open end,
sun will produce running water.

I Saw My Picture, There Was A Ghost

I saw my picture with the old dog
sun-faded, taken awhile ago.
There was a ghost
behind a berm of sand.
There can be no wind that is not harsh
for that is the nature of wind.
It foretold that we would
fade away in the sun.
She may have known this
at the time.
Camels, she'd said there would be camels
following us.
I never knew if she was joking or not.
Avanti, the ghost of my old dog
sits ye down amongst the beach-grass.
I never knew if she was joking
she led the chorus of laughter.
Avanti, the old dog
always quick with announcements
invited a guest conductor.
She led the chorus as if she were joking.

I traced out your shape in the air,
I poked my finger through it, yes it seems like you,
I mean, I can stick my head right through the air that you
occupy. And you can do the same to me.

I trace your basic form, medium head, graceful slope of
long arms, to the tall
red meadow grass, your feet were lost in the abundant thistle,
this being spring, and a rainy one at that.

I traced out your torso, I knew it well,
stepped around and molded front and back. From this angle I
saw circling crows through your hair, blue crows, the pair
yapping as they moved out of your ear hole. I did see a
black heifer watering itself in your vortex.

I never bothered with your environment, nor your thought processes
although, at this moment, small yellow canaries are darting about
in the river trees and you told me many times that the river
trees were alders and quite unreliable.

A problem with the idea of dealing with ghosts, how many of
these tricks are true? You say the drowned will
surface after nine days at the weed bed, by the river's bend.
Oh, Oh, the wind told me that, can I believe it came from
you, let me check my tracing, yes, there is wind, small birds,
tall grass and a pair of crows, yapping.

Prayer to the Wind-walker, Mother

They come from any direction, the wind-walkers do, disguised
as yellow fall leaves, graceful in a downward spiral of death,
as birds, yellow canaries, dancing in the leaves, a movement
gives a shape, it looks to me as if wind-walkers are in the alder trees
       by the cabin.
The wind-walkers rise up through the branches at every sunny
       opening.
Into the terrible consequences of finishing without closure.
Wind driven debris-men from far past highways,
late night robbers who congregate at the Outskirts Motel,
driven like wind spirits, walking with no destination
pinballs between colored lights
happy to dance on the orb,
sure of their ability to snatch with their feet.
Wind-walker monkeys, Mother, are you there amongst that bunch?
You came with the wind today, cool to the touch
and now, Mother, perhaps it is to honor you,
my fascination with colored lights.
On the bad highway, the neon sign at the Outskirts Motel
announces in angry sequences, Vacancy, Vacancy, Vacancy. We
       pull in.

I will point out to you the illuminated parts of what I see in the dark,
        empty places
you will have to fill in from your own experience.
It's just occurred to me that I'm the last station at the end of our line,
        Coney Island,
last stop before the sea, home in language of my clan, it ends with
        me.
Is the last station on the line
empty at four in the morning?
Coney Island by the sea. Just outside the last station
a howling wind off the sand keeps the birds still in the
eaves. Newspapers huddle, are plastered against the shuttered
steel fronts of the carnival.
Is there anyone in the last station on the line, any trail
musk even, a dried rubber boot pattern, any sign, occurrence of
        accident, any
difference in the shade of light creeping in from the east, the wind is
        more biting
now,
more zealous in its search for any semblance
that would dare step out
of the last station at the end of the line.

The close-up visions are the worst. How near things are and yet
with my yardstick eyes I see the specter of death, creeping in
creeping out, a body so powerful with intention it does not wish to
        be seen. The
ability to measure time for your own personal accounts, you see
        things that you only
suspected. The cat watches the door intently, I watch her eyes, perhaps
        cats have
that kind of vision, can see things that creep. Hunters and trackers,
        let's say. And
what must this do to your heart. You see with measurement. Another
        organ has
developed, the not-heart, just the cold calculation that this is what it
        really is and no
preparation could prepare you for this moment.

On Turning 80

Every time I reach a certain age
I forget about the bell
and how it bongs the time away.
I hear it century after century
its echo only fades
when we reach the year of the late 70s.
I must admit that I am astonished
by the silence
as if a snow miles deep
now covered my autumn world.
Bong!

They say you can see stars in the daytime if you are in a hole in the
       earth that drops
thousands of feet into the dark and cold of clay. From this icy depth
       they say you
can see the stars. I saw them in the eyes of this stranger to me, my
       mother. "Follow
me," she said, beckoning promises that I will see the stars. I came to
       the end of the
canoe dock for some reason, and stepped off over the water, into the
       dark chill, still
seeking the stars.

The Holy Ghost Whispered to me in the Birth Canal

"then the moon was gone
leaving only the hole
then it was gone"
leaving only my light in the water

ABOUT THE AUTHOR

Bill Bradd was born to farm people in Muskoka, Ontario, Canada. As a young man, he drifted, worked the oil fields in Alberta and bartended in New York City. In 1967 he arrived in California where he lived for a time in the Big Sur area, then migrated further north, became an active member of a thriving community of writers and artists in the North Coast area of Mendocino and has remained there ever since. He has published two books of poetry, one of which, *The Kingdom of Old Men*, was named one of the best books of the year by *Poetry Flash*; a book of essays/memoirs; and three spoken word CDs. He was a major contributor to an oral history project for the Mendocino County Historical Society, interviewing more than 100 people born before 1900 which provided a unique view into the history of the area. The project resulted in the book, *Mendocino County Remembered*. His work has appeared in *ZYZZYVA*, *Beloit Poetry Journal*, *Ashanti*, *Winter*, *Arts Canada* and other journals and magazines. One of his stories, "The Whistle Stop," was included in an A.R.S. Brevis/ACT event in San Francisco where actors read selected short stories. He was an editor of *The Mendocino Review* and Ten Mile River Press, which was awarded a National Endowment grant for poetry publications. He also received a Canada Council Grant and taught for many years in the California Poets in the Schools Program. He is the Poet Laureate of Ten Mile River.

NOTE: The following Spoken Word CDs are available directly from
www.billbradd.com

> *I Tried To Sing In My Grandfather's Voice*
> *New Work*
> *Continent of Ghosts*